ELIJAH OF BUXTON

by
Christopher Paul Curtis

Teacher Guide

Written by
Terry L. Romer

Note

The Scholastic Press hardback edition of the book, © 2007 by Christopher Paul Curtis, was used to prepare this guide. The page references may be different in other editions. Novel ISBN: 978-0-439-02344-3

Please note: Please assess the appropriateness of this book for the age level and maturity of your students prior to reading and discussing it with them.

ISBN 978-1-60539-090-1

To order, contact your local school supply store, or—
Novel Units, Inc.
P.O. Box 97
Bulverde, TX 78163-0097

Web site: www.novelunits.com

Copyright infringement is a violation of Federal Law.

© 2008 by Novel Units, Inc., Bulverde, Texas. All rights reserved. No part of this publication may be reproduced, translated, stored in a retrieval system, or transmitted in any way or by any means (electronic, mechanical, photocopying, recording, or otherwise) without prior written permission from ECS Learning Systems, Inc.

Photocopying of student worksheets by a classroom teacher at a non-profit school who has purchased this publication for his/her own class is permissible. Reproduction of any part of this publication for an entire school or for a school system, by for-profit institutions and tutoring centers, or for commercial sale is strictly prohibited.

Novel Units is a registered trademark of ECS Learning Systems, Inc.
Printed in the United States of America.

Table of Contents

Skills and Strategies

Critical Thinking
Main idea/supporting details, compare/contrast, summarizing

Literary Analysis
Character analysis, figurative language, author's purpose, story map, foreshadowing

Comprehension
Cause/effect, sequencing, predicting, conflict

Vocabulary
Context clues, word maps

Writing
Character journal, personal writing, poetry

Across the Curriculum
Map skills, history, research

Genre: young-adult historical fiction

Setting: Buxton, Ontario, Canada

Point of View: first person

Themes: coming of age, facing fears, hope, triumph, family, friendship, freedom

Conflict: person vs. person, person vs. society

Tone: adventurous, humorous, serious

Summary

Elijah, the first freeborn child in a settlement of freed slaves, is a sensitive child. Elijah and his best friend Cooter have several comical adventures, each usually ending with Elijah running off scared and screaming. Although naïve, Elijah proves his importance to the community by helping neighbors and through his involvement in school, church, and the community. Life takes a turn when 11-year-old Elijah is kidnapped and finds himself in pursuit of a thief. The thief has stolen money intended to buy freedom for a former slave's family. As the novel progresses, Elijah matures and rises to the challenge of unimaginable hardships, including the death of a friend. *Elijah of Buxton* introduces readers to a little-known piece of history: 1860 pre-emancipation America and the Canadian haven for runaway slaves in Buxton, Ontario, Canada.

About the Author

Christopher Paul Curtis lives in Windsor, Ontario, Canada, only miles from the setting of *Elijah of Buxton*. Born in Michigan, Mr. Curtis says that while writing this book, he and Elijah became "close friends." He explains: "When I'd go to the library to write, it was as if [Elijah] was anxiously waiting for me, waiting to tell me about his life, his worries, his adventures." Winner of both the Newbery Honor and the Coretta Scott King Award, Christopher Paul Curtis is the author of *The Watsons Go to Birmingham* and *Bud, Not Buddy*. Some of his best-known novels are both comical and deeply moving, blending fictional accounts of families with factual events. He and his wife have two children.

Background Information

Buxton, Canada: The Canadian town of Buxton is located just 40 miles from Detroit, Michigan. During the 1860s (the time period in which the novel is set) Buxton served as a community for runaway slaves and their children, a place where blacks could govern themselves away from the dangers of pre-emancipation America. As described in the Author's Note, the Settlement ranged in population at its height from 1,500 to 2,000 escaped and freed people. The success of Buxton resulted from the determination of its mostly freed black residents and the strict codes instituted by its founder, Reverend William King. Buxton's students included native Canadian children, since the school developed a stellar reputation among families in the area.

Slavery in America: Twelve million Africans were brought to America as slaves between 1600 and 1900. Slaves were used as laborers by their white owners primarily in the South, on tobacco plantations and in other areas of agriculture. There were no laws regarding slavery in pre-emancipation America. Consequently, harsh living conditions led to resistance, and slave owners often employed violence to sustain sunrise-to-sunset gang labor. Slaves were provided minimal housing, food, and medical care. They had little opportunity to improve their quality of life. Beginning in the 1750s, sentiment regarding the social evil of slavery grew, leading to the movement to end slavery. Following the Civil War, slavery became illegal.

Characters

Elijah Freeman: main character and protagonist; 11-year-old boy who is the first freeborn child in a community of former slaves; thoughtful and naïve

Ma and Pa: Elijah's parents

The Preacher/The Right Reverend Deacon Doctor Zephariah Connerly the Third: self-proclaimed preacher who attempts to ensnare Elijah in his flimflam activities

Mr. Leroy: a freed slave who is saving his money to buy his wife and children out of slavery

Cooter: Elijah's best friend; described as dimwitted

Mrs. Bixby: Cooter's domineering mother

Mrs. Holton: runaway slave raising two daughters; Her husband dies at the hands of slave owners.

Mr. Segee: owns stables, horses, and Old Flapjack, Elijah's favorite mule

Emma: Elijah's sensitive and annoying classmate; chosen to welcome escaped slaves to Buxton

Mrs. Chloe, Kamau, and Hope/Too-mah-ee-nee: family of slaves captured while escaping

Mr. Highgate: resident of Buxton who is shot by the Preacher while traveling to America

Mr. Benjamin Alston: American black who helps Mr. Highgate after he is shot

Mr. Travis: Elijah's demanding school and Sunday school teacher

Miss Carolina, Mr. Waller, the Miss Duncans, Mr. Polite, Mrs. Guest: hardworking residents of Buxton

The Taylors: former slave family that has escaped to Buxton from America

Initiating Activities

It is important for students to understand the context of the Civil War and slavery before reading this novel. Make sure students fully understand these concepts in order to make comprehension of the characters' motivations and actions easier. (To begin, see the Background Information section on page 4 of this guide). Use discretion and sensitivity when discussing slavery and its relationship to racial injustices.

Use one or more of the following to introduce the novel:

1. Discussion: Introduce the concepts of pre-Civil War slavery and slaves' struggles to become free. Use books, the Internet, and videos to emphasize the hardships endured by slaves in the United States.

2. Geography: Using a classroom map, consider the possible routes taken by slaves to reach Buxton, Canada after they escaped or were freed. In small groups, have students chart and label a route. Display the products in the classroom.

3. Research: Have students find information about Frederick Douglass and John Brown. Have students create time lines of their lives and place them on the classroom wall to demonstrate how they were instrumental in the anti-slavery movement.

4. Literary Analysis: Discuss dialect and its impact on the reading and writing of dialogue. Choose examples from the book, and ask the students to decipher the words out of context. Then use the words in the context presented in the novel.

5. Prereading: Have students complete the Getting the "Lay of the Land" activity on page 19 of this guide.

6. Predicting: Have students begin the Prediction Chart on page 20 of this guide. Students will continue this activity as they read the novel.

Vocabulary Activities

1. Mix and Match: Write vocabulary words on individual index cards. Write definitions on other index cards, making sure there are enough for each student to have one word and one definition card. Have students move around the room attempting to match their words with others' definition cards. After all cards are paired, use the dictionary to see if the pairings are correct. Suggested words: commence, berserk, peculiar, familiarity, oddities, dexterity, prestidigitation spectacles, abolitionist, and hankering.

2. Dictionary Race: Divide the class into groups of three or four students. Provide a dictionary to each group. Write vocabulary words on the board or overhead projector, and ask groups to find the definitions. The group that finds the definitions first wins the race.

3. Vocabulary Symbols: Have students complete the Vocabulary Symbols activity on page 21 of this guide using a list of selected vocabulary words.

4. Vocabulary Sentences: Read aloud two or three pages from the novel. Ask students to write down the adjectives they hear, and then have them define the words they listed. Have each student use each word in an original sentence to share with the class.

5. Words In Use: Assign one vocabulary word to each student. As homework, s/he must use the word in an everyday situation at school or home and report how s/he used the word.

Chapters 1–4

Two details have shaped Elijah's identity in Buxton. First, he is the first freeborn child in Buxton, the Canadian settlement for former slaves. Second, when he was a baby, Elijah threw up on the famous Frederick Douglass as Mr. Douglass was giving a speech. These two facts about Elijah are well known in Buxton. Elijah also has a talent for "chunking stones," or throwing stones to hit and catch fish—a talent that is viewed with interest by the shady Preacher, who swindles Elijah out of several fish. Elijah and other black students in Buxton are escorted from school when slavers are suspected in the area. That night, Elijah finds a riderless horse. The Preacher shows up with a fancy holster and an expensive-looking pistol after searching unsuccessfully for the owner of the horse.

Vernacular
afore
waren't
conjure
brogans
rile
scallywags

Vocabulary
mysterious
commence
prolonged
fragile
fretting
blaspheming
berserk
tithing
tolerable

Discussion Questions

1. What does Elijah mean by "...there're lots of things that Cooter sees as being mysterious that most folks understand real easy" (pp. 1–2)? *(Cooter is not a very smart boy.)*

2. How does the Preacher describe himself? How does he seem to use his abilities? *(He says he is educated and intelligent. He uses his wits to take advantage of Elijah and anyone who will believe his stories.)*

3. When do Ma and Elijah first discover their differing opinions about being "fragile"? What views of this quality do they each have? *(When Elijah was very young, Ma picked up a snake and scared him. Ma thinks running from a little snake is cowardly, but Elijah thinks it is sensible.)*

4. How does Ma get even for the frog trick? *(She puts a snake in the cookie jar to scare Elijah.)*

5. What do people say about Frederick Douglass' visit to Buxton? For whom is the story most embarrassing? *(The famous man bounced Elijah around during a speech, and Elijah threw up all over Mr. Douglass. This story has embarrassed Elijah all his life.)*

6. What two contradictory things does Ma tell Elijah about adults? How does he feel about her advice? *(She tells him to respect what adults say and not to believe everything you are told. Elijah is confused and frets about not understanding the adult world.)*

7. What is the meaning of the Buxton Creed? How does the creed benefit the community? *(Everyone looks out for and helps everyone else in the Settlement. By cooperating, the residents of the tiny settlement are able to be self-sufficient and to weather hardships.)*

8. How does Elijah's rock-chunking help him and others? How might this skill be important in the plot of the novel? *(He throws rocks at fish and catches them. Then he shares the food with his family and neighbors. Answers will vary.)*

9. Why do the townspeople make up stories or "pretty up" tales? *(It is a source of entertainment since they do not have much else to do but gossip and talk. Also, they have lived hard lives and these tales provide some escape from their painful memories.)*

10. **Prediction:** How did the Preacher get his silver-plated pistol?

Supplementary Activities

1. Anecdote: Choose a story from your childhood, such as Elijah's experience with Frederick Douglass. Write a "prettied up" version of the story as the townspeople of Buxton might tell it.

2. Service Project: Elijah chunks stones to catch fish and gives them to members of his community. Participate in a class discussion about how today's students can help their communities. Come up with a service idea together, and put it into action.

3. Skit: Dramatize the dialogue between the Preacher and Elijah in Chapter 3, emphasizing the humor in the Preacher's math.

4. Dialect: As a class, discuss how the dialect used in this book adds to the richness of language. In groups of four, see how many examples of dialect you can find in Chapters 1–4. Examples might be sensical, atall, waren't, gunn, cain't, axed, afeared, terrorfied, n'em, tragical, borned, chawing, ain't, and pesty.

5. Literary Devices: Use the Metaphors and Similes chart on page 22 of this guide to write at least one simile and one metaphor from this section. Include an interpretation for each example. Continue adding to your chart as you read each section. Examples: **Simile**— "[Mules] have a way of rocking you gentle like a baby in a crib" (p. 36); **Metaphor**— chunking stones: work of the Devil (p. 37)

Chapters 5–8

The Settlement has many regulations regarding how houses and land must be kept. Everyone works to meet these community goals, including Elijah. He completes chores in the Settlement to contribute, along with other residents. One resident is Mr. Leroy, a hardworking man trying to save enough money to buy his wife and children out of slavery. Elijah enjoys working beside Mr. Leroy but avoids his schoolteacher, Mr. Travis, an old-fashioned, strict taskmaster who teaches the children respect for their superiors. There are brief times for amusement, such as when the Preacher talks Elijah into secretly going to the carnival with him. There, Elijah discovers many con artists and charlatans, and he questions the Preacher's motives for taking him along.

Vernacular
antsy
persnickety
haint
tuckered
jawing

Discussion Questions

1. Why does Mrs. Brown have "spells"? (*She lost her only baby and suffers from mental problems and depression due to the loss.*)

2. What are the Settlement rules about houses? Why are these rules necessary? (*They must be ten paces from the road, have a white fence, stoop, and flower garden. Answers will vary, but the rules contribute to the success of the colony, economically and otherwise.*)

3. Give examples of how Elijah's family helps others in the community. What kind of bond does this cooperation create? (*Elijah helps Mr. Leroy chop wood, and he chunks stones to catch fish for people. His father helps Mrs. Halton clear stumps. Ma cooks for other people. Residents are buoyed by the support they receive.*)

Vocabulary
plaguing
familiarity
contempt
suspicious
oddities
calliope
dexterity
reputation
rendered
ambush

4. Why does Mr. Leroy toil long hours at such back-breaking work? What does this say about him? *(He is trying to save money to buy his family out of slavery. He loves and misses his family and thus makes sacrifices for them.)*

5. What is Mr. Leroy's philosophy of life? *(You cannot be timid or expect bad things to happen, or they will.)*

6. What is the best way to learn something, according to Elijah? Is this the way you learn best? *(He thinks learning by experience is the best method. Answers will vary.)*

7. What lesson is Mr. Travis trying to teach? *("Familiarity breeds contempt," meaning that people who feel too comfortable around their superiors do not treat them with due respect. Cooter misinterprets the phrase to mean "family breeding contest.")*

8. Why does Elijah's remark make Mr. Leroy so angry? *(Mr. Leroy was called this term when he was being abused as a slave in the South.)*

9. What does the Preacher want Elijah to do? How does Elijah feel about the offer? *(He wants Elijah to sneak out at night and go to a carnival with him. Elijah is suspicious and wary because he knows his parents wouldn't let him go, but he agrees because it is an opportunity for adventure.)*

10. What does Elijah discover about MaWee? *(He finds out that "MaWee" is really a white student from his school.)*

Supplementary Activities

1. Literary Techniques: At the beginning of Chapter 7, Elijah foreshadows coming events. Find and record two other examples of foreshadowing from previous chapters.

2. Creative Thinking: Create a carnival sideshow attraction like the ones in the book. Consider the "unreal" atmosphere and attitude involved in such activities. Illustrate and summarize your sideshow idea in a brief paragraph, and then act it out.

3. Writing: Pretend you are Elijah, and write a letter of apology to Mr. Leroy for offending him.

4. Literary Devices: Continue adding to your Metaphors and Similes chart. Examples: **Simile**—"The fish bones crackled and snapped in his mouth like dry corn in a mill" (p. 76); **Metaphor**—Mrs. Holton: unfortunate soul (pp. 71–72)

Chapters 9–12

Elijah sneaks off to the carnival with the Preacher, where they discover a boy who is being treated like a slave by the carnival people. The Preacher wants to see the mesmerist and tells Elijah to pay attention to learn how a flimflam works. Elijah chunks stones for the carnival owner, but the Preacher decides not to sell Elijah to the carnival for his skills. After leaving the carnival, the Preacher returns, gets the slave boy MaWee, and brings him to the Settlement. A new family of escaped slaves comes to the community and are welcomed in the traditional ways. The Duncan sisters discover that the new woman, Alice Duncan, is their long-lost sister.

Vernacular
mesmerist
rigmarole
flimflam
rapscallion
lollygagging
speechifying

Vocabulary
prestidigitation
dumbstruck
nonsense
pendulum
skittish
precious
respectable
tolling

Discussion Questions

1. How does the author use the five senses to describe the carnival? *(He describes Elijah using his eyes and ears to discover the strangeness of the place.)*

2. Why is Elijah afraid of the mesmerist? What does this say about Elijah? *(He thinks the mesmerist will make him float into the sky. He is gullible and naïve.)*

3. What prediction can you make from the title of Chapter 10, "Meeting the *Real* MaWee!"? *(Predictions will vary but might include thoughts that there are at least two boys playing the character of MaWee.)*

4. How do the carnival employees treat MaWee? Does he mind this treatment? Why or why not? *(He is overworked and beaten by the carnival people. He is treated like a slave. He does not mind this treatment because he has no place else to go.)*

5. Why did the Preacher suddenly leave the carnival? *(He saw the real sign that was racially inflammatory.)*

6. Predict where the Preacher is going after leaving Elijah at home. What is he going to do? *(Answers will vary but might include that he is going back to the carnival to help MaWee.)*

7. Why is MaWee upset after being freed? *(He has been taken away from the only life and security he has known. He is confused because he never thought of himself as a slave.)*

8. Why does the community allow Emma Collins to greet newly arrived slaves? *(She charms people and makes them see that the Settlement is a safe place where they will not be hurt.)*

9. How does Pa welcome the new family? Why does he emphasize the things that he does? *(He points to the air, the land, and the people and tells them how beautiful and free they are. Answers will vary, but he is probably sensitive to their feelings of gratitude for life and the promise of a home because he was once an escaped slave himself.)*

10. What is the importance of the Liberty Bell in Buxton? *(Former slaves in Pittsburgh saved to give the community a gift representing freedom. The bell is rung every time new person(s) who were formerly slaves enter the commuity.)*

11. Why are the Duncans waiting to tell Mrs. Taylor that she is their sister? Could you exhibit such restraint in an exciting situation? *(Mrs. Taylor has been through too much and has a sick baby, so she doesn't need more stress at the moment. Answers will vary.)*

Supplementary Activities

1. Writing: Using your five senses, write a description of an unusual place you have been, such as a carnival.

2. Social Studies: Research the original Liberty Bell in Pennsylvania. How is it similar to the bell in Buxton? Present your detailed findings using the Venn diagram on page 23 of this guide.

3. Research: Look up Buxton, Canada on the Internet. What is being done to keep the memory of the Settlement alive? Create a brochure encouraging tourists to visit Buxton.

4. Literary Devices: Continue adding to your Metaphors and Similes chart. Examples: **Simile**— "That way if I started floating, the Preacher could have pulled me, long home like a kite" (p. 120); **Metaphor**—mesmerist: old humbug (p. 122)

Chapters 13–16

Elijah picks up a letter from America informing Mrs. Holton of tragic news: Her enslaved husband has died due to abuse by his owner. Mrs. Holton had saved money to buy her husband's freedom, so she gives Mr. Leroy $2,000 in gold. He can now save his own family from slavery. Pa worries about the wily Preacher's offer to help Mr. Leroy, so Pa insists that the Preacher take Mr. Highgate with him to America to seek help in freeing Mr. Leroy's family.

Vernacular
druthers
daft
punctuating
hankering

Vocabulary
shied
hefted
refuge
missive
retaliation
remunerate
eavesdropping
abolitionists
admirable
misery
vipers

Discussion Questions

1. What does "...his mind isn't amongst us anymore" (p. 186) mean? (*Mr. Butler's brain was injured, and he does not understand much or think clearly.*)

2. Why is a letter from America usually bad news? How does the letter make Elijah feel? (*It is generally about a death, sickness, or sale of an enslaved loved one. It makes Elijah sad.*)

3. What is the educational requirement for each adult in the Settlement? What does this reveal about the community? (*They are required to learn to read and write. The community values literacy and education for all.*)

4. How did Mrs. Holton's husband die? (*He was whipped to death by his owner.*)

5. What stories don't the adults want the children to hear? Why are they protective of their children? (*They are talking about their memories of being slaves. Answers will vary, but the stories include violence and atrocities unknown to their children and perhaps too frightening for their comprehension.*)

6. Was Ma's mother's anger justified when she hit her daughter? (*Answers will vary, but Ma's mother was angry that Ma had the opportunity to escape to Canada and did not do so.*)

7. Who is Mrs. Holton quoting when she talks about strength? What does the statement mean? (*Ma; Answers will vary, but the statement "Something inside so strong gunn keep you flying" [p. 211] is a message of hope.*)

8. What does Elijah think about all week? How does Elijah improve on his original idea? *(All he can think about is what words should be carved in the wooden sign above Mrs. Holton's door. He makes the message more concise and more positive.)*

9. What is as good as repayment to Mrs. Holton? Why does she feel this way? *(hearing the Liberty Bell toll when Mr. Leroy's family gets to town; Mrs. Holton lost her husband to slavery, so she will feel gratification and justice by helping Mr. Leroy free his family.)*

10. What help does Mr. Leroy need from Pa? *(He needs to connect with the Underground Railroad or a person capable of helping escaped slaves.)*

11. Do you trust the Preacher? *(Answers will vary, but most students will not trust him and will think he plans to steal Mr. Leroy's money.)*

12. **Prediction:** What will become of the Preacher and Mr. Leroy's money?

Supplementary Activities

1. Predicting: Read the foreshadowing at the end of Chapter 16 where Pa says, "I wish it waren't so, but I just ain't feeling good 'bout this" (p. 237). Write your predictions about what is going to happen.

2. Research: In small groups, research the Underground Railroad. Study this important movement and its involvement in the process of relocating slaves. Either write a play to be presented to the class or develop projects that describe locations in the route of the Underground Railroad.

3. Literary Devices: Continue adding to your Metaphors and Similes chart. Examples: **Similes—** "I feels like I's swimming I's looking through so many tears" (p. 208); "...my mama's arm uncoil like a rattling-snake..." (p. 209); **Metaphor—**Canada: gates of Heaven (p. 210)

Chapters 17–20

The Preacher shoots Mr. Highgate and runs off with Mr. Leroy's money. Mr. Leroy "kidnaps" Elijah and takes him to Michigan to hunt for the Preacher and his stolen money. After making Elijah promise to either get the money back for his wife and daughter or shoot the Preacher, Mr. Leroy suffers a heart attack and dies.

Vernacular
cleaving
tussling
bushwacked
trifled

Vocabulary
regards
concentrating
gasping
kidnapper
intention
examination
sullied
ferry
nudge

Discussion Questions

1. What news does Cooter bring Elijah? Why does Elijah feel guilty about what has happened? *(Mr. Highgate is hurt, and the Preacher is not with him. He told Mr. Leroy that the Preacher could be trusted with his money, and now the Preacher and the money are gone. Elijah believes the whole thing is his fault.)*

2. Who is the kidnapper? What qualities make his "victim" a desirable companion? *(The kidnapper is Mr. Leroy. Elijah can read, is comfortable talking to white people, and has a keen mind.)*

3. What does Mr. Leroy plan to do? How does this knowledge make Elijah feel? *(He plans to hunt for the Preacher in Michigan and either get his money back or kill him. Elijah feels less than brave.)*

4. Why will Elijah have to do the thinking for himself and Mr. Leroy? What does this show about Elijah? *(Mr. Leroy is so upset about what has happened that he cannot think straight. Elijah is maturing.)*

5. Why does Elijah think this might be the last time he hugs his parents? *(He knows he is headed into danger and may not return.)*

6. What happens to Mr. Leroy? How does Elijah feel about the situation? *(He collapses and slides off the horse. He is afraid and heartbroken.)*

7. Whom does Mr. Leroy think he is talking to as he dies? *(his son 'Zekial)*

8. What is the promise Elijah must keep? Does he intend to keep it? Why or why not? *(He promises Mr. Leroy that he will get the money back. Elijah intends to honor his promise. Answers will vary, but Elijah is obviously a person of integrity.)*

9. **Prediction:** How will Elijah handle the slavers and their dog?

Supplementary Activities

1. Writing: Reread Elijah's situation at the end of Chapter 20. Then write a paragraph entitled "A Promise I Would Keep." Describe an important obligation you have honored, or one that you would honor if necessary.

2. Speaking/Listening: In small groups, talk about making difficult decisions. Begin the discussion with the decisions Elijah has had to make and his motivations for his actions at this point in the novel. Share your group's opinions with the class.

3. Health: As a class, discuss basic CPR techniques. Discuss how the procedure could have helped Mr. Leroy if Elijah had known how to assist him. Watch an instructional video demonstrating this life-saving technique.

4. Literary Devices: Continue adding to your Metaphors and Similes chart. Examples: **Similes**— "Mr. Leroy grabbed his left arm and started breathing like he'd just been chopping oaks" (p. 282); "...a growned person you know is hard as nails" (p. 283); **Metaphors**—milk: lump of butter in [Elijah's] belly (p. 275); wealthier men: bigger fish to fry (p. 279)

Chapters 21–24 and Author's Note

In his search for the Preacher and Mr. Leroy's money, Elijah enters a barn where he finds a group of escaped slaves and the body of the Preacher, who has been killed by the slavers. Elijah only has time to rescue the baby girl, Hope, and take her back to Buxton where he welcomes her with his father's beautiful words about freedom. The author discusses the history of Buxton at the end of the novel. In the Author's Note, Christopher Curtis reveals three details of *Elijah of Buxton* that are based on fact: Frederick Douglass and John Brown did visit; a girl did escape as Elijah's mother did; and the Liberty Bell was rung the way it was in the novel.

Vocabulary
swooningest
brook

Vocabulary
shackles
rafters
gourd
fierce
calculated
agitating
conscience
posse
jarring
plaguing
whining

Discussion Questions

1. What sounds and smells does Elijah experience in the barn? Which sense does Elijah trust the most? *(He hears tails swishing, hoofs scraping, and animals breathing. He smells horses, straw, goats, and something unidentifiable; He trusts his sight most.)*

2. Who are the people in the barn? What connection does Elijah make between these people and what he smells? *(They are runaway slaves who have been recaptured. He identifies the strange smell as their fear.)*

3. What does Elijah remember about abolitionists? *(They risk their lives to free slaves.)*

4. What is Elijah going to do about the slaves? *(Answers will vary but will likely involve Elijah trying to rescue the slaves.)*

5. What circumstances are overwhelming Elijah? *(Mr. Leroy has died. The Preacher is dead. The atmosphere and conditions of the slaves in the barn are too much for Elijah to comprehend.)*

6. Why do you think Mrs. Chloe tells Elijah how much the baby loves him? *(Answers will vary, but she wants Elijah to save her child.)*

7. Why can't Elijah go back to Buxton and bring help? *(It will take too long to do that. The slaves will already be gone.)*

8. How does Elijah compare his conscience to the cookie jar snake? *(They both are going to be with him for a long time, except his memory of leaving the slaves behind will be more difficult to forget about.)*

9. Why does Elijah lie about the baby looking like a sister of his? *(He is giving Mrs. Chloe an excuse to give the baby to him.)*

10. How does Elijah welcome the baby to freedom? *(He repeats his father's words about the beauty of being free.)*

11. For what will Elijah be most remembered in Buxton? *(He will be remembered for rescuing Hope.)*

12. When Reverend King began the Settlement, which people came to live there? *(Fifteen slaves he had inherited and six escaped slaves came there.)*

13. What does the author say are the two reasons the Settlement succeeded? What is the most likely source of the first reason for success? *(It succeeded thanks to courage, determination, and strict rules. The residents had courage and determination because they wanted to remain free.)*

14. What kind of school was the Academy at Buxton? What does its reputation reveal about the community? *(It was of such high caliber that even white Canadian families sent their children there. The Settlement strove for excellence in academics to ensure future prosperity and to develop a sense of pride.)*

15. Give examples of events that actually happened in Buxton. What do these details reveal about the genre of this novel? *(Frederick Douglass and John Brown did visit; a girl did escape as Elijah's mother did; the Liberty Bell was rung the way it was in the novel. The novel is historical fiction because it blends fictionalized characters and plot details with facts.)*

Supplementary Activities

1. Writing: The author uses the senses of hearing and smell to describe the barn. Write a description of a place using sensory details.

2. Drama: In small groups, choose a scene from the last section of the novel to dramatize. Present your scene to the class.

3. Predicting: Record predictions about the town of Buxton and what happened there in the years following those written about in this novel. The Internet site buxtonmuseum.com (active at time of publication) is a good resource for checking your predictions.

4. Literary Elements: Continue adding to your Metaphors and Similes chart. Examples: **Simile**—"...your mind and brain seize up like a pump in the winter" (p. 320); **Metaphors**— smell in the stable: fear (p. 303); slaves: haints (p. 294)

5. Research: Find three additional facts about Buxton that could be added to the Author's Note, and present your findings in class.

Post-reading Discussion Questions

1. How does the author reveal the horrors of slavery in *Elijah of Buxton*? *(He reveals slavery's horrors through the relation of stories from former slaves now living in Buxton, through Elijah's encounter with the family of captured runaway slaves, through the sadness of loved ones lost to slavery, and by showing families split apart and longing for their lost relatives.)*

2. What lessons does Elijah learn through his experiences in this novel? *(He learns the value of friendship, compassion, and the importance of people helping one another. He also learns that down deep he is truly strong, not "fragile," as he has always been led to believe.)*

3. How would this novel have been different without the character of the Preacher? *(As the antagonist of the story, the novel would have had little conflict without the Preacher. Through his actions and influence, Elijah finds opportunities for bravery and maturity.)*

4. To what does the Settlement owe its success in the novel? *(The Settlement owes its success to its founder, Reverend King, to the community's rules, but mostly to the hard work, determination, spirit, and cooperation of its residents—former slaves who value and protect their freedom.)*

5. What did you learn about pre-emancipation America, the Underground Railroad, and Buxton while reading this novel? *(Answers will vary, but students should exhibit basic knowledge of the practice of pre-Civil War slavery in the United States, the idea that people could be bought and sold, the role played by the Underground Railroad in helping slaves escape, and the history of the Settlement in Buxton, Canada.)*

6. Mr. Leroy is an important character in this story. Explain his importance in Elijah's growth. *(Mr. Leroy's hard work for money to buy his family makes him a good role model for Elijah. Mr. Leroy's determination to regain his family teaches Elijah how precious the freedom he takes for granted is to others. Additionally, the climax of the story, in which Elijah proves his strength and bravery, comes about through his promise to the dying Mr. Leroy.)*

7. What do you predict Elijah's future will be? *(Answers will vary but may include a good education and continued involvement in the success of the Settlement.)*

8. What does the Liberty Bell symbolize? *(It represents freedom for the former slaves as they enter Buxton.)*

9. Why do you think the author named Mrs. Chloe's baby Hope? *(The baby is a symbol of hope for a better life that all the people of Buxton hold. Her name also represents her mother's hope for her life.)*

10. Discuss the growth from "fragile" to strong that Elijah experiences in this novel. *(Elijah evolves from a sensitive, timid child who is easily frightened and runs from problems to a brave young man who faces challenges and overcomes adversity. He learns that being afraid does not mean he is a coward. He displays courage by trying to keep his promise to Mr. Leroy and by inadvertently saving Hope. He uses good judgment while with Mr. Leroy and later in approaching Mr. Alston.)*

11. What do you think is the most humorous event in the novel? Why? *(Answers will vary but could include the story of Elijah and Frederick Douglass, the hoop snake story, the Preacher's swindling of Elijah's fish, and many others.)*

12. What makes Cooter effective as a sidekick? *(Answers will vary but could include that he is dimwitted but lovable, and he is loyal to Elijah. Cooter also provides comic relief in the novel.)*

13. What literary elements does the author use effectively in this novel? *(Answers will vary, but students should cite particular instances of figurative language, dialect, point of view, characterization, foreshadowing, and humor.)*

14. The plot of the novel does not actually begin until after several mini-adventures have been told. What is the purpose of this storytelling technique? *(The mini-adventures develop the characters and demonstrate their individual qualities, define Buxton's setting and history, and prepare the reader for Elijah's act of courage in the climax.)*

Post-reading Extension Activities

Writing

1. Create a journal entry Elijah might have written at any point during this novel. Include his description of events and his feelings as he experiences those events.

2. Pretend you are a book reviewer for the local newspaper, and write a one-page review of this novel. Discuss in detail the positive and negative aspects of the book, and assign a rating to the novel.

Art

3. Design a new cover for this book. What character or scenes do you want to depict? Be sure to write a two-paragraph teaser for the book jacket that does not give away the ending of the novel.

4. Create a bookmark based on *Elijah of Buxton*. Display this bookmark with your classmates' work. Bookmarks are usually made 2.5" X 7.5" on cardstock paper with simple, but striking and colorful images on the front and information on the back, including the book's title, author, publisher, and a teaser quote from the novel. Creative additions include a tassel or a special shape other than rectangular.

5. Illustrate one scene from the book. Use any medium you choose, such as paint, collage, or other art materials. Display your work in the classroom.

Critical Thinking

6. Complete the Effects of Reading chart on page 24 of this guide. Which parts of the novel made you think or laugh? Which parts made you want to take action or touched your heart? List each in the appropriate box.

7. Use the A Character's World activity on page 25 of this guide to draw parallels between yourself and the characters in *Elijah of Buxton*. What things that are important to the characters are also important to you?

8. Complete the Story Pyramid on page 26 of this guide.

9. Fill out the Venn Diagram on page 27 of this guide to compare and contrast the lives of freed slaves in the South with those of freed slaves in Buxton.

Research

10. Research present-day Buxton, Ontario, Canada, including its culture, festivals and events, nearby natural wonders, population, economy, and more. Present your findings in the form of a brochure or a classroom display.

Assessment for *Elijah of Buxton*

Assessment is an ongoing process. The following ten items can be completed during the novel study. Once finished, the student and teacher will check the work. Points may be added to indicate the level of understanding.

Name _____ Date _____

Student   **Teacher**

_____   _____   1. Write a ten-question final test for *Elijah of Buxton*. Make sure the test reflects the vocabulary, comprehension, and language skills you have learned throughout your study of the novel. The test may be in multiple-choice or short answer format. Be sure to include an answer key for your questions.

_____   _____   2. Participate in a "Vocabulary Bee" in which the teacher gives you a vocabulary word and you respond with the definition as used in the novel.

_____   _____   3. Write a concise summary of the book using at least ten vocabulary words.

_____   _____   4. Rewrite the ending of this story. Be consistent with what you have learned about the characters and the historical viewpoint of the novel.

_____   _____   5. Complete the Cause and Effect chart on page 28 of this guide.

_____   _____   6. Re-read the examples of foreshadowing on pages 93, 106, 133, and 260 of the novel. Choose one, and explain the situation it foreshadowed later in the book.

_____   _____   7. Prepare an illustrated time line detailing Elijah's trip to the carnival with the Preacher. Include the sights Elijah sees, his feelings about them, and the people he and the Preacher meet. End by envisioning how the Preacher gets MaWee to Buxton and how MaWee feels about his rescue.

_____   _____   8. As your teacher reads quotations from the book, write the names of the characters being quoted.

_____   _____   9. Write a journal entry from Elijah's point of view that tells about events of this story in the correct sequence. Include Elijah's feelings about other characters and the situations in which he finds himself.

_____   _____   10. Complete the Understanding Values activity on page 29 of this guide.

Getting the "Lay of the Land"

Directions: Prepare for reading by answering the following short-answer questions.

1. Who is the author?

   _____

2. What does the title suggest to you about the book?

   _____

   _____

   _____

   _____

3. When was the book first copyrighted?

   _____

4. How many pages are there in the book?

   _____

5. Thumb through the book. Read three pages—one from near the beginning, one from near the middle, and one from near the end. What predictions can you make about the book?

   _____

   _____

   _____

   _____

   _____

6. What does the cover suggest to you about the book?

   _____

   _____

   _____

   _____

Prediction Chart

Directions: Record your predictions as you read the novel using the chart below.

What characters have we met so far?	What is the conflict in the story?	What are your predictions?	Why did you make these predictions?

Vocabulary Symbols

Directions: Write each vocabulary word in the correct column below.

Noun	Verb	Adjective or Adverb
♣	❀	▲
❖	■	✖
❊	♣	♥
♦	❁	❀
❀	▲	❊
▲	♦	❁
■	❖	♦
❁	✖	♣
♥	❊	■
✖	♥	❖

Find sets of words with the same symbols. For example, the three words written beside the ♥ form a set. On a separate sheet of paper, write a sentence that includes each set of words.

Metaphors and Similes

A **metaphor** is a comparison between two unlike objects. For example, "he was a human tree." A **simile** is a comparison between two unlike objects that uses the words *like* or *as*. For example, "the color of her eyes was like the cloudless sky."

Directions: Complete the chart below by listing metaphors and similes from the novel, as well as the page numbers on which they are found. Identify metaphors with an "M" and similes with an "S." Translate the comparisons in your own words, and then list the objects being compared.

Metaphors/Similes	Ideas/Objects Being Compared
1. Translation:	
2. Translation:	
3. Translation:	

Compare/Contrast

Directions: Use the Venn diagram below to compare and contrast the Liberty Bell in Pennsylvania with the Liberty Bell in Buxton, based on your research.

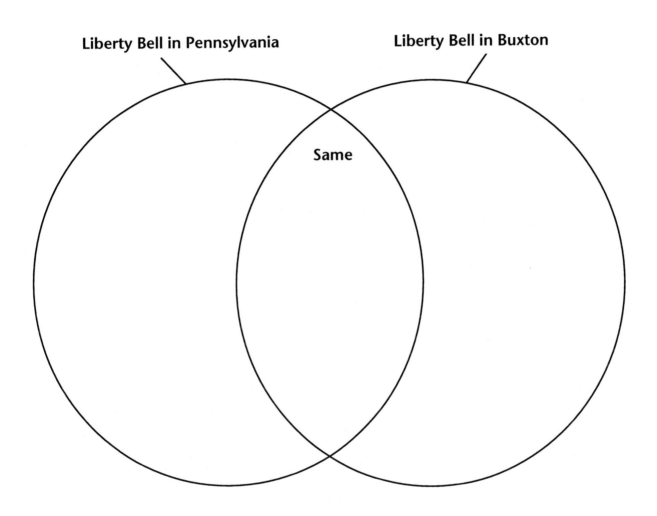

Liberty Bell in Pennsylvania

Liberty Bell in Buxton

Same

Effects of Reading

Directions: When reading, each part of a book may affect you in a different way. Think about how parts of the novel affected you in different ways. Did some parts make you laugh? cry? want to do something to help someone? Below, list one part of the book that touched each of the following parts of the body: your head (made you think), your heart (made you feel), your funny bone (made you laugh), or your feet (spurred you to action).

Your head	Your heart

Your funny bone	Your feet

A Character's World

Directions: You may be able to draw parallels between a character's world and your own. Write a character's name in the blank. Describe that character's world. Then describe a related situation or event from your own world.

_____'s World

_____

_____

_____

My World

_____

_____

_____'s World

_____

_____

_____

My World

_____

_____

_____

_____'s World

_____

_____

_____

My World

_____

_____

_____

_____'s World

_____

_____

_____

My World

_____

_____

_____

Story Pyramid

Directions: Using the pyramid, write words or phrases to summarize the story.

Line 1: One word that gives the setting

Line 2: Two words that identify the two main characters (in order of their appearance)

Line 3: Three words that explain the problem

Line 4: Two words that describe character #1; two words that describe character #2

Line 5: Two characters that interact with character #1; three characters that interact with character #2

Line 6: Six words that explain the resolution of the conflict

Line 7: Seven words that summarize your impression of the book

1 _____

2 _____ _____

3 _____ _____ _____

4 _____ _____ _____ _____

5 _____ _____ _____ _____ _____

6 _____ _____ _____ _____ _____ _____

7 _____ _____ _____ _____ _____ _____ _____

Venn Diagram

Directions: Fill out the Venn diagram comparing and contrasting life for the freed slaves in the South and in Buxton.

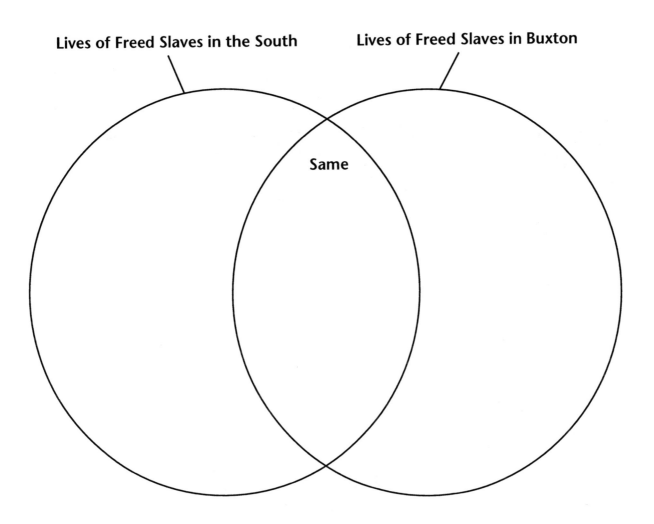

Lives of Freed Slaves in the South

Lives of Freed Slaves in Buxton

Same

Cause and Effect

Directions: Write four events from the story, and then list the effect of each event.

Cause	Effect

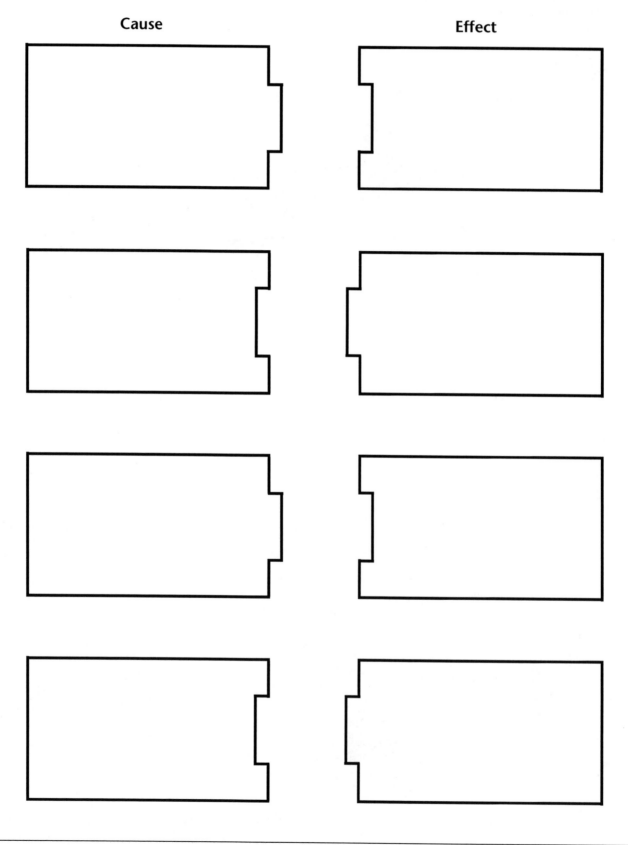

Understanding Values

Values represent people's beliefs about what is important, good, or worthwhile. For example, most families value spending time together.

Directions: Think about the following characters from the novel and the values they exhibit. What do they value? What beliefs do they have about what is important, good, or worthwhile? On the chart below, list each character's three most important values, from most important to least. Be prepared to share your lists during a class discussion.

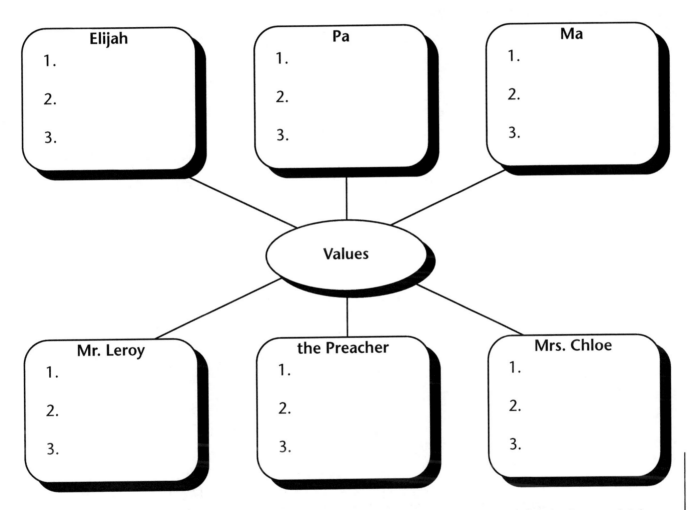

After you have finished the chart and participated in the class discussion, think about which character seems to have values most like your own. Write a paragraph that explains why you chose this character.

Linking Novel Units® Lessons to National and State Reading Assessments

During the past several years, an increasing number of students have faced some form of state-mandated competency testing in reading. Many states now administer state-developed assessments to measure the skills and knowledge emphasized in their particular reading curriculum. The discussion questions and post-reading questions in this Novel Units® Teacher Guide make excellent open-ended comprehension questions and may be used throughout the daily lessons as practice activities. The rubric below provides important information for evaluating responses to open-ended comprehension questions. Teachers may also use scoring rubrics provided for their own state's competency test.

Please note: The Novel Units® Student Packet contains optional open-ended questions in a format similar to many national and state reading assessments.

Scoring Rubric for Open-Ended Items

3-Exemplary	Thorough, complete ideas/information Clear organization throughout Logical reasoning/conclusions Thorough understanding of reading task Accurate, complete response
2-Sufficient	Many relevant ideas/pieces of information Clear organization throughout most of response Minor problems in logical reasoning/conclusions General understanding of reading task Generally accurate and complete response
1-Partially Sufficient	Minimally relevant ideas/information Obvious gaps in organization Obvious problems in logical reasoning/conclusions Minimal understanding of reading task Inaccuracies/incomplete response
0-Insufficient	Irrelevant ideas/information No coherent organization Major problems in logical reasoning/conclusions Little or no understanding of reading task Generally inaccurate/incomplete response

Notes

Notes